UNDERSTANDING
THE HOLY SPIRIT
MADE EASY

Understanding the Holy Spirit Made Easy
©2018 Rose Publishing, LLC

Rose Publishing, LLC
P.O. Box 3473
Peabody, Massachusetts 01961-3473 USA
www.hendricksonrose.com

Contributing author: Len Woods

Cover and layout design by Cristalle Kishi.

Photos and illustrations provided by Shutterstock.com.

Printed in the United States of America
010718VP

CONTENTS

Frequently Asked Questions

"*The Spirit-filled life is not a special, deluxe edition of Christianity. It is part and parcel of the total plan of God for His people.*"

A. W. TOZER

WHO IS THE HOLY SPIRIT?

Before his death, resurrection, and return to heaven, Jesus promised his disciples that he would send them "another advocate to help you and be with you forever—the Spirit of truth. The world cannot accept him, because it neither sees him nor knows him. But you know him, for he lives with you and will be in you" (John 14:16–17).

Three things are worth noting in Jesus' promise:

- Firstly, "another advocate" means *another of the same kind*. In other words, as he discussed his own departure, Jesus promised to send his followers a helper who would be like him.

- Secondly, Jesus consistently referred to the Spirit as a "he" not an "it." This means that the Spirit is a person—not a vague power or impersonal force.

- Thirdly, Jesus assured his disciples this divine, personal Spirit of truth would never leave them. The Holy Spirit is the Christian's constant companion and advocate. The Holy Spirit is God living in those who believe in and follow Jesus!

What Happened at Pentecost?

After Jesus ascended into heaven, his disciples were gathered in Jerusalem to pray and celebrate the Jewish festival of Pentecost. The sound of a great rushing wind filled the house they were in. The image of tongues of fire touched each disciple. By the power of the Holy Spirit, the disciples spoke in different languages (or "in tongues"). The crowd who had gathered in the city for Pentecost witnessed this power and some were utterly amazed, but others mocked the disciples. Nevertheless, 3,000 people believed and were baptized.

This incident was the first of many miraculous events that proved the promises of Jesus to be true: "You will receive power when the Holy Spirit comes on you" (Acts 1:8) and this Holy Spirit will live with you and be in you (John 14:17).

(Read about the events of Pentecost in Acts 2:1–41.)

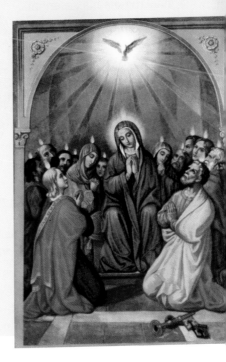

THE TRINITY

To understand who the Holy Spirit is we need to understand who God is. This means we need to learn what God reveals in his Word about his triune nature. From the Bible, we can glean the following truths:

God is spirit.

- This means his essential nature is immaterial or non-physical.

- John 4:24

God is one.

- This means that there aren't multiple gods, and that God's nature or essence is perfect unity.

- Deuteronomy 6:4; Isaiah 44:6–8; 45:5

The one and only God exists as three distinct persons: God the Father, God the Son, and God the Holy Spirit.

- God is triune in nature. He is one, yet three. This is what people mean when they speak of *the Trinity*. For our finite minds, this "three-in-oneness" is an impossible-to-comprehend mystery, but the Bible clearly reveals God as a Trinity of divine Persons existing in perfect unity.

- Matthew 3:16–17; 28:18–19; 2 Corinthians 13:14; Ephesians 4:4–6

Each of the persons of the Trinity is fully God—and not to be confused with the other persons of the Trinity.

The Father is God.

- 1 Corinthians 8:6; Ephesians 4:4–6

The Son is God.

- John 1:1–5, 14; 10:30–33; 20:28; Hebrews 1:6–8; Philippians 2:9–11

- Also see these passages about Jesus' deity: Isaiah 7:14; 9:6; John 1:1, 18; 8:58, 59; 10:30; Acts 20:28; Romans 9:5; 10:9–13; Colossians 1:15, 16; 2:9; Titus 2:13; Hebrews 1:3, 8; 2 Peter 1:1; 1 John 5:20

Holy Spirit or Holy Ghost?

The term *Holy Ghost* is used in some older Bible translations, such as the King James Version (KJV). But the underlying Greek and Hebrew words translated as *ghost* or *spirit* are the same. This means that *Holy Spirit* and *Holy Ghost* are just different English translations.

The Holy Spirit is God.

- Acts 5:3–4; 2 Corinthians 3:16–17 (compare with Exodus 34:34).

With that quick overview, we can answer the question:

Who is the Holy Spirit?

The Holy Spirit is God! The Holy Spirit is the third Person of the Trinity.

"Go and make disciples of all nations, baptizing them in the name of the Father and of the Son and of the Holy Spirit." Matthew 28:19

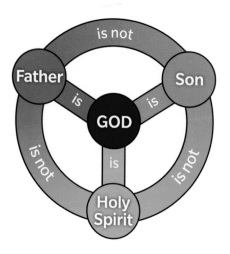

This diagram, often called the *Shield of the Trinity*, illustrates how each of the three Persons of the Trinity is God, but each is not identical to the other.

Divine Attributes of the Trinity

DIVINE ATTRIBUTE	FATHER	SON	HOLY SPIRIT
Eternal	Romans 16:26–27	Revelation 1:17	Hebrews 9:14
Creator of all things	Psalm 100:3	Colossians 1:16	Psalm 104:30
Omnipresent (capable of being all places at once)	Jeremiah 23:24	Ephesians 1:23	Psalm 139:7
Omniscient (knows all things)	1 John 3:20	John 21:17	1 Corinthians 2:10
Wills and acts supernaturally	Ephesians 1:5	Matthew 8:3	1 Corinthians 12:11
Gives life	Genesis 1:11–31; John 5:21	John 1:4; 5:21	Romans 8:10–11; John 3:8
Strengthens believers	Psalm 138:3	Philippians 4:13	Ephesians 3:16

ACTIVITIES OF THE HOLY SPIRIT

In the past, the Holy Spirit:

- Created the world (Genesis 1:2; Psalm 104:30).

- Inspired and superintended the human authors of Scripture (2 Peter 1:21).

- Conceived Jesus (Luke 1:35).

- Resurrected Christ (Romans 8:11; 1 Peter 3:18).

In the present, the Holy Spirit:

Seals

Like a seal of authenticity, the Holy Spirit marks us as God's property.

"You also were included in Christ when you heard the message of truth, the gospel of your salvation. When you believed, you were marked in him with a seal, the promised Holy Spirit." Ephesians 1:13

Regenerates

Apart from this spiritual rebirth, we cannot come alive to God (Ephesians 2:1–5).

"Flesh gives birth to flesh, but the Spirit gives birth to spirit." John 3:6

Indwells

When we put our trust in Christ, the Holy Spirit of the living God actually takes up residence in our lives!

"If the Spirit of him who raised Jesus from the dead is living in you, he who raised Christ from the dead will also give life to your mortal bodies because of his Spirit who lives in you." Romans 8:11 (See also 1 Corinthians 6:19.)

Convicts

The Holy Spirit convinces people of their need to repent from sin and to look to Christ for righteousness.

"When [the Holy Spirit] comes, he will convict the world of its sin, and of God's righteousness, and of the coming judgment." John 16:8 NLT

Guides

When life is dark and the way is vague, the Holy Spirit is our leader.

"But when he, the Spirit of truth, comes, he will guide you into all the truth. He will not speak on his own; he will speak only what he hears, and he will tell you what is yet to come." John 16:13

The Temple of the Holy Spirit

In Old Testament times, the temple (and the tabernacle before it) was the place where God's special presence resided. It was the holy sanctuary where God's people met with their holy God.

In the New Testament, all believers together—the church—are called God's temple. As the apostle Paul says:

- *"Don't you know that you yourselves are God's temple and that God's Spirit dwells in your midst?"* (1 Corinthians 3:16).

Not only are believers together the temple, but our individual bodies are also called temples:

- *"Do you not know that your bodies are temples of the Holy Spirit, who is in you, whom you have received from God?"* (1 Corinthians 6:19)

The Spirit of God who once dwelt in the temple in ancient times now indwells believers today. Knowing this truth should encourage us to "honor God with [our] bodies" (1 Corinthians 6:20). Our bodies—both individually and together as the body of Christ, the church—should not be used for sinfulness and immorality, but to honor God by being receptive to the work of the Spirit whose presence makes us holy.

Advocates

The Holy Spirit is the 24/7 counselor and defender of Jesus' followers.

"I will ask the Father, and he will give you another advocate to help you and be with you forever." John 14:16

Teaches

The Holy Spirit shows us what's right, what's wrong, and how to live.

"The Holy Spirit, whom the Father will send in my name, will teach you all things and will remind you of everything I have said to you." John 14:26

Intercedes

Knowing the will of God and the desires of our hearts, the Holy Spirit speaks to God on our behalf.

"In the same way, the Spirit helps us in our weakness. We do not know what we ought to pray for, but the Spirit himself intercedes for us through wordless groans." Romans 8:26

Gives Assurance

In big and small ways, the Holy Spirit confirms that we belong to God and that he is working in us.

"The Spirit himself testifies with our spirit that we are God's children." Romans 8:15–16

Empowers

We are not called to live for God in our own limited strength. The Holy Spirit is our infinite power source.

"But you will receive power when the Holy Spirit comes on you; and you will be my witnesses in Jerusalem, and in all Judea and Samaria, and to the ends of the earth." Acts 1:8 (See also Ephesians 5:18.)

THE HOLY SPIRIT IN THE LIFE OF JESUS

The perfect unity of the Trinity is seen in the inseparable relationship between God the Son and God the Holy Spirit. At every stage of Jesus' life and ministry we see the presence and power of the Spirit.

We see the Holy Spirit in . . .

Prophecies about Christ.

The Jewish prophet Isaiah said that the Spirit of God would rest on the coming Messiah (*Christ*, in Greek), granting him wisdom, understanding, and knowledge (Isaiah 11:2–3). In another prophecy about God's anointed servant, Isaiah records God saying, "I will put my Spirit on him" (Isaiah 42:1).

The Forerunner's Life.

John the Baptist was chosen by God to serve as the forerunner of the Messiah. A forerunner is like an "advance man." It was John's job, therefore, to announce to Israel that the promised Messiah had finally come. Because he was selected for this hugely important role, John was filled with the Holy Spirit while still in his mother's womb (Luke 1:15)!

When John grew up and began preparing people for the arrival of Jesus, he spoke of Jesus as one who would baptize repentant people "with the Holy Spirit and fire" (Matthew 3:11).

Jesus' Birth.

The Gospels of Matthew and Luke both speak of the Holy Spirit's role in causing Mary, a virgin, to conceive

the Christ. "The Holy Spirit will come upon you, and the power of the Most High will overshadow you; and for that reason the holy Child shall be called the Son of God" (Luke 1:35; see also Matthew 1:18–20). Exactly how the virgin birth of Christ happened is a biological mystery, but that it happened is an unmistakable biblical teaching. Mary was not pregnant as a result of human agency. Jesus was conceived supernaturally, by the Spirit of God.

In this miraculous moment, the second person of the Trinity took on sinless human nature. In his birth Jesus didn't suddenly gain personhood—he has always existed. But God the Son did become human (John 1:1, 14).

Shortly after Jesus' birth, Simeon, a Spirit-filled man at the temple in Jerusalem, recognized the infant in Mary's arms as Israel's Messiah (Luke 2:25–27).

Jesus' Baptism.

The Gospels record that immediately after Jesus was baptized by John, "heaven was opened, and he saw the Spirit of God descending like a dove and alighting on him" (Matthew 3:16; see also Mark 1:9–11; Luke 3:21–22). This baptism officially kicked off Jesus' earthly ministry, and it functioned as an anointing ceremony.

In ancient times, new prophets, priests, or kings were anointed with oil. The way in which the oil was poured on their heads and allowed to drip down on their bodies symbolized that they were set apart for God's special use. By pouring out the Spirit on Jesus at his baptism, God was indicating that he, Jesus, was God's special, chosen servant (Luke 4:18; Acts 10:38).

Jesus' Ministry.

Luke notes that Jesus was consistently "full of the Holy Spirit" and "led by the Spirit" (Luke 4:1; see also verse 14). In other words, the Spirit continually guided and empowered Jesus as he went about his earthly mission. When his followers reported a successful mission trip, Jesus was "full of joy through the Holy Spirit" (Luke 10:21).

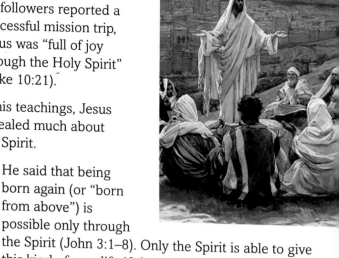

In his teachings, Jesus revealed much about the Spirit.

- He said that being born again (or "born from above") is possible only through the Spirit (John 3:1–8). Only the Spirit is able to give this kind of new life (John 6:63).

- He talked of the Spirit being God's generous gift (John 3:34).

- He said that those the Spirit indwells will seem to have "rivers of living water" flowing from within them (John 7:38–39).

- The night before his death, Jesus assured his troubled followers that the Spirit would be their constant helper—that he would guide them and instruct them in the truth (John 14:17–26; 15:26; 16:13).

Commissioning His Disciples.

After his resurrection, Jesus urged his followers to wait for the coming Spirit (Luke 24:49), because he—the Holy Spirit—would enable them to be powerful witnesses of the gospel (Acts 1:8; see also Mark 13:11). In his final charge, just before returning to heaven, Jesus commanded that every new disciple be baptized "in the name of the Father, and of the Son, and of the Holy Spirit" (Matthew 28:19).

Do you see? It's impossible to talk about the birth, life, death, and resurrection of Jesus without also talking about the Holy Spirit!

"When the Spirit came to Moses, the plagues came upon Egypt, and he had power to destroy men's lives; when the Spirit came upon Elijah, fire came down from heaven; when the Spirit came upon Gideon, no man could stand before him; and when it came upon Joshua, he moved around the city of Jericho and the whole city fell into his hands; but when the Spirit came upon the Son of Man, He gave His life; He healed the broken-hearted."

DWIGHT L. MOODY

SYMBOLS OF THE HOLY SPIRIT

By definition, anything that's *spiritual* is non-physical, immaterial, invisible. This obviously includes the Holy Spirit. We can't see the Spirit of God with our physical eyes, but we can see the effects of the Spirit. It's for this reason that the Bible uses various symbols—often common, earthly objects—to describe who the Holy Spirit is and what he does.

Deposit

In saying that God "put his Spirit in our hearts as a deposit" (2 Corinthians 1:22), the apostle Paul used a commercial term. The Greek word *arrabon* means "down payment, pledge, or first installment." The presence of the Spirit in our lives is a guarantee that God will finish the work he has started in us.

> " . . . being confident of this, that he who began a good work in you will carry it on to completion until the day of Christ Jesus."
>
> **PHILIPPIANS 1:6**

Dove

After Jesus was baptized, witnesses watched the Spirit of God descend on him from heaven "like a dove" (Matthew 3:16; Mark 1:10; Luke 3:22; John 1:32). This doesn't necessarily mean that the Spirit became an actual dove, only that he resembled one.

What's the symbolism here? How is God's Spirit "like a dove"?

- Doves are the universal symbol of peace. It's only fitting then that Jesus, the "prince of peace" (Isaiah 9:6) who came to help sinners experience "peace with God" (Romans 5:1) would be crowned, as it were, with peace at the beginning of his public ministry.

- Doves are also, as Jesus said in Matthew 10:16, a symbol of purity. How fitting that the "Holy" Spirit would be likened to a creature considered innocent and pure.

Wind

In John 3, Jesus uses a play on words to inform Nicodemus, a Jewish religious leader, that the *Spirit* of God is like *wind*. The Greek word, *pneuma*, which is translated as *Spirit, can also be translated wind or breath*. The Lord's point is that while we can't actually see wind, we *can* feel a cool breeze or watch a flag whip wildly. As the wind is unpredictable—suddenly kicking up or swirling or changing direction—so the Spirit acts in ways we can't predict. Some days are still—we can't sense even the hint of a "spiritual breeze." Other days, the Spirit moves with sudden, astonishing power, almost like a wind shear. Still other times, like a favorable tailwind to a sailor, the Spirit brings us to wonderful destinations.

Seal

In 2 Corinthians 1:22, Paul uses a rich, descriptive phrase to help us understand the person and work of the Spirit. He calls the third Person of the Trinity God's "seal" on believers (see also Ephesians 1:13; 4:30).

What does it mean that God *seals* Christians with his Spirit? In ancient times, seals were used to show ownership. Think of a rubber stamp used to mark a book as being "From the Library of Winchester B. Winthrop IV" or a cattle brand marking a prize bull as the property of "Crooked Z Ranch." Seals also served as a means of security and protection. Remember how Pilate told his guards to secure the grave of Jesus by "putting a seal on the stone" (Matthew 27:64–66)?

When we speak of the Spirit as a seal, we mean that God owns Christians, and that believers are eternally safe and secure.

Oil

In the Old Testament, newly chosen prophets, priests, and kings were routinely anointed with oil (Exodus 40:11–15; Leviticus 8:30; 1 Samuel 10:1–10; 16:13). This ceremony conveyed an important truth to everyone watching: the person upon whom the oil was poured was being set apart for God's holy use. Anointed officials were to live as servants of the one true God. They were to rely on the Spirit of God, not their own power (Zechariah 4:1–14).

The New Testament uses this same anointing imagery to speak of Christians (compare Acts 10:38 with Acts 1:8; 2 Corinthians 1:21; 1 John 2:20). It is the Holy Spirit who anoints us, setting us apart for God's service.

Fire

In the Old Testament, the presence of God is often symbolized by fire.

- God speaks to Moses out of a burning bush (Exodus 3:2).

- The Israelites know that God is among them because of the blazing fire in or over their tabernacle (their portable worship center)—see Exodus 40:38.

- The Israelites are guided through the wilderness at night by "a pillar of fire" (Numbers 14:14).

- Sacrifices acceptable to God are sometimes consumed by fire from heaven (Leviticus 9:24; 1 Kings 18:38–39).

In the New Testament, when the Holy Spirit was poured out on those who had put their faith in Jesus, Acts 2:3 records that witnesses saw "tongues of fire" coming "to rest on each of them." This demonstrated that God now resided in the hearts of believers!

Fire can also be a symbol of judgment, and the Spirit came to convict the world of sin and righteousness and judgment (John 16:8–11). Fire also purifies, and the Holy Spirit came to make us holy (Romans 15:16; 1 Peter 1:2).

Water

One of the more prominent biblical symbols for the Holy Spirit is water. The best example? In ancient times, at the end of the Feast of Tabernacles, Israel's high priest would pour out (near the altar) a pitcher of water drawn from the Pool of Siloam. This was such a happy occasion—with singing and celebrating and hopeful anticipation of Messiah's future reign (Zechariah 14:16–21)—that Israel's rabbis declared that people who had never witnessed this ritual did not know the true meaning of joy!

During his earthly ministry, Jesus seized upon this ancient tradition to declare his unique ability to quench the deepest thirsts of the human heart (John 7:37–38). He promised to give the Holy Spirit to those who trusted him. And he said that the indwelling Spirit would be like "rivers of living water" flowing from within believers. Perhaps picking up on this idea, the apostle Paul described joy, peace, and hope as qualities that would overflow from the life of a Spirit-led Christian (Romans 15:13; Galatians 5:22–23).

Fountains, streams, wells—all of these watery images are used to demonstrate the work of the Spirit. Water cleanses and refreshes. It gives life, and when harnessed correctly, provides great power.

Clothing

After his crucifixion and resurrection, Jesus appeared multiple times to his most devoted followers. On one of those occasions, he told his disciples to take the good news of forgiveness "to all nations." But first, he said, "stay in the city until you have been clothed with power from on high" (Luke 24:49).

"Power from on high" is a clear reference to the Holy Spirit (John 14:16; 16:7–15; Acts 1:8). But what an interesting description! According to Jesus, the Spirit is something like clothing. Without clothing, we are naked and vulnerable. When we try to live without the power of the Spirit, we are spiritually naked and vulnerable.

NAMES OF THE HOLY SPIRIT

Some people think of the Holy Spirit as impersonal, rather like a force—the energy or power of God. This is probably because:

- The Scriptures confirm the powerful nature of the Holy Spirit.

- He is called the *power of God and Spirit of might.*

And yet, unlike an impersonal force, the Holy Spirit has personhood:

- He can be lied to (Acts 5:3–4).

- He can be grieved (Ephesians 4:30).

- He has a name (Matthew 28:19).

Others see the Spirit almost as a feeling—the deep affection that often is experienced among God's people. Maybe this is because . . .

- The Scriptures call him the Spirit of grace, of mercy, and of comfort.

- However, he is also called the Spirit of truth and justice, indicating that he is more than simply a warm fuzzy feeling we get when we pray and worship together.

Still others regard the Holy Spirit as the mind, the intellect, behind creation.

- To be sure, he is the Spirit of wisdom and understanding.

- However, he is more than a cosmic computer that keeps God's plans and purposes on course.

Each of these views is limited, giving an incomplete picture of who the Holy Spirit is. Studying the names of the Spirit found in the Bible helps us get a fuller, more balanced idea of who the Spirit is and how he operates. With such an understanding, we're able to worship and serve God in deeper and richer ways.

Advocate
(Helper, Comforter)

SCRIPTURE

"I will ask the Father, and he will give you another advocate to help you and be with you forever."
John 14:16

MEANING

The Holy Spirit comforts, counsels, defends, and gives strength.

TAKEAWAY

The Holy Spirit is our strength and comfort. We are to turn to him when we are in trouble and when we are weak, being assured that he intercedes (pleads our case before God) with and for us.

DID YOU KNOW?

Paraclete is the Greek word behind this name. It refers to someone called alongside to strengthen and fight on behalf of another.

God

SCRIPTURE

"Ananias, how is it that Satan has so filled your heart that you have lied to the Holy Spirit and have kept for yourself some of the money you received for the land? Didn't it belong to you before it was sold? And after it was sold, wasn't the money at your disposal? What made you think of doing such a thing? You have not lied just to human beings but to God." Acts 5:3–4

MEANING

The Holy Spirit is the Third Person of the Trinity. He is God.

TAKEAWAY

The Holy Spirit is not a thing, a force, or mere power. He is not an "it." He is personal, and we are to worship and obey him as God.

DID YOU KNOW?

God is one in his essence, but three in Person.

Good Spirit

SCRIPTURE

"Teach me to do your will, for you are my God; may your good Spirit lead me on level ground." Psalm 143:10

MEANING

God's Spirit will teach and lead us in all that is good.

TAKEAWAY

The Holy Spirit is God's good gift to us for help in the present. We are not alone in the world. Christ's very own Spirit is with us to work all things for our good.

DID YOU KNOW?

Goodness is one of the fruits of the Spirit in Galatians 5:22.

Holy Spirit

SCRIPTURE

"Therefore go and make disciples of all nations, baptizing them in the name of the Father and of the Son and of the Holy Spirit." Matthew 28:19

MEANING

God is Spirit and that Spirit is holy. He is the Spirit of holiness.

TAKEAWAY

The same Holy Spirit given to us for life is given to make us holy as well.

DID YOU KNOW?

The Greek word for holy, *hagios*, refers to something or someone who is sacred, set apart for a divine purpose, and pure.

Lord

SCRIPTURE

"Now the Lord is the Spirit, and where the Spirit of the Lord is, there is freedom." 2 Corinthians 3:17

MEANING

Like Jesus and the Father, the Holy Spirit is also addressed and worshiped as Lord.

TAKEAWAY

The Holy Spirit is our Lord. The lordship of the Spirit means that we are to obey him and not grieve him.

DID YOU KNOW?

When we follow the leading of the Spirit as our Lord, we find true freedom.

Power of the Most High

SCRIPTURE

"The angel answered, 'The Holy Spirit will come on you, and the power of the Most High will overshadow you. So the holy one to be born will be called the Son of God." Luke 1:35

MEANING

The Holy Spirit has all the power of God because he is God.

TAKEAWAY

By the Spirit, God can accomplish things in and through us that we could never do ourselves.

DID YOU KNOW?

The Greek word for power, *dunamis*, is the word from which we get our English word dynamite.

"When it is a question of God's almighty Spirit, never say, 'I can't.'" Oswald Chambers

The Spirit

SCRIPTURE

"Flesh gives birth to flesh, but the Spirit gives birth to spirit." John 3:6

MEANING

The Holy Spirit is sometimes simply called "the Spirit."

TAKEAWAY

The Spirit is necessary for all spiritual life and growth.

DID YOU KNOW?

The spiritual life is not trying hard to do good, it is trusting Jesus to live through us by surrendering control of our wills to the indwelling Spirit of God.

Spirit of Adoption

SCRIPTURE

"The Spirit you received does not make you slaves, so that you live in fear again; rather, the Spirit you received brought about your adoption to sonship. And by him we cry, 'Abba, Father.'" Romans 8:15

MEANING

It is by God's Spirit that we are adopted as God's children.

TAKEAWAY

We become God's children by the work of the Holy Spirit. As the Spirit opens and changes our hearts, we become part of God's family. Because of the Spirit's saving work, God becomes our heavenly Father.

DID YOU KNOW?

The Aramaic word used by Jesus (and that's mentioned in Romans 8:15) is *Abba*, which means "Daddy" or "Papa."

Spirit of Christ

SCRIPTURE

"You, however, are not in the realm of the flesh but are in the realm of the Spirit, if indeed the Spirit of God lives in you. And if anyone does not have the Spirit of Christ, they do not belong to Christ." Romans 8:9

MEANING

The Spirit of Christ is the Holy Spirit who led Jesus Christ and was promised to believers.

TAKEAWAY

The Holy Spirit always acts in ways that honor Christ, just as Christ always acted in ways that honored the Father. Jesus has shared the Spirit who filled and animated him with those who believe in him.

DID YOU KNOW?

In the perfect community that is the Trinity, the Father, Son, and Holy Spirit endlessly and selflessly honor one another.

Spirit of Counsel

SCRIPTURE

"The Spirit of the Lord will rest on him—the Spirit of wisdom and of understanding, the Spirit of counsel and of might, the Spirit of the knowledge and fear of the Lord." Isaiah 11:2

MEANING

Because of the Spirit, God's anointed Servant—Jesus Christ the Messiah—has all the divine guidance of heaven when he comes.

TAKEAWAY

The same Spirit of counsel who filled and guided Jesus is available to us.

DID YOU KNOW?

Jesus is called the Wonderful Counselor (Isaiah 9:6).

Just as the Holy Spirit led Jesus, he leads us to truth as our Counselor (Luke 4:1; John 14:26).

Spirit of the Father

SCRIPTURE

"For it will not be you speaking, but the Spirit of your Father speaking through you." Matthew 10:20

MEANING

The Spirit of God is sent by the Father to enable believers to imitate the Father and do the will of the Father (John 15:26; Ephesians 5:1).

TAKEAWAY

The Spirit of the Father and of Jesus has been sent to us by them.

DID YOU KNOW?

The Spirit carries out the will of the Father and the Son—and empowers us to do likewise.

Spirit of the Fear of the Lord

SCRIPTURE

"The Spirit of the LORD will rest on him . . . the Spirit of the knowledge and fear of the LORD." Isaiah 11:2

MEANING

The Spirit's nature is to be reverent and respectful.

TAKEAWAY

The Holy Spirit will always lead us to revere God. It is the Holy Spirit who inspires this attitude in us.

DID YOU KNOW?

The "fear of the Lord" is not a sense of terror, but one of reverence and honor. It's a deep sense of who God is and who we are in relation to him. It's also "the beginning of knowledge" (Proverbs 1:7).

Spirit of Freedom

SCRIPTURE

"Therefore, there is now no condemnation for those who are in Christ Jesus, because through Christ Jesus the law of the Spirit who gives life has set you free from the law of sin and death." Romans 8:1

MEANING

The Holy Spirit sets believers in Christ Jesus free from the bondage of sin and death.

TAKEAWAY

Along with the apostle Paul, we too can declare that "where the Spirit of the Lord is, there is freedom" (2 Corinthians 3:16–17).

DID YOU KNOW?

Early in Jesus' ministry, he read from a prophecy in the scroll of Isaiah declaring his mission to be: "to proclaim freedom for the prisoners . . . and to set the oppressed free" (Luke 4:18; Isaiah 61:1).

Spirit of Glory

SCRIPTURE

"If you are insulted because of the name of Christ, you are blessed, for the Spirit of glory and of God rests on you."
1 Peter 4:14

MEANING

When we live faithfully in a hostile world, the Holy Spirit causes us to be radiant.

TAKEAWAY

The Spirit enables us to glorify Christ no matter what obstacles we face in this world.

DID YOU KNOW?

The Holy Spirit is shaping our lives into the glorious pattern of Christ.

Spirit of God

SCRIPTURE

"Now the earth was formless and empty, darkness was over the surface of the deep, and the Spirit of God was hovering over the waters." Genesis 1:2

MEANING

The Holy Spirit is the Spirit of the triune God.

TAKEAWAY

As Jesus explained to the Samaritan woman at the well, "God is spirit, and his worshipers must worship in the Spirit and in truth" (John 4:24).

DID YOU KNOW?

The Spirit of God was instrumental in the creation of the universe (Genesis 1:2).

Spirit of Grace

SCRIPTURE

"I will pour on the house of David and on the inhabitants of Jerusalem the Spirit of grace and supplication."
Zechariah 12:10 NKJV

MEANING

God's Spirit is a merciful spirit.

TAKEAWAY

We come to know God's grace only when the Spirit opens our hearts. Jesus accomplished the work of grace for us on the cross, but it is the Spirit who applies that grace to us by giving us faith.

DID YOU KNOW?

Supplication means to ask humbly. The Holy Spirit helps us have a humble attitude as we come to God in prayer, asking him for our needs.

Spirit of Justice

SCRIPTURE

"He will be a spirit of justice to the one who sits in judgment, a source of strength to those who turn back the battle at the gate." Isaiah 28:6

(See also Micah 3:8; Matthew 12:18.)

MEANING

The Spirit of God brings conviction and justice.

TAKEAWAY

God's Spirit discerns truth from error and divides good from evil.

DID YOU KNOW?

Jesus said the Holy Spirit would convict and judge the world (John 16:8).

Spirit of Knowledge

SCRIPTURE

"The Spirit of the LORD will rest on him . . . the Spirit of the knowledge." Isaiah 11:2

MEANING

God's Spirit is all-knowing. His understanding and wisdom are infinite.

TAKEAWAY

The Spirit does not lead to confusion but to true knowledge (1 Corinthians 14:33).

DID YOU KNOW?

Jesus is the Messiah that Isaiah prophesied; therefore, Jesus possessed the fullness of the Spirit of knowledge.

Spirit of Life

SCRIPTURE

"Because through Christ Jesus the law of the Spirit who gives life has set you free from the law of sin and death."
Romans 8:2

MEANING

The Holy Spirit is life-giving.

TAKEAWAY

Just as physical life requires breath, so spiritual life requires God's Spirit.

DID YOU KNOW?

Jesus said he is life (John 14:6). The Spirit is the giver of this new life in Jesus (John 6:63).

Spirit of the Living God

SCRIPTURE

"You show that you are a letter from Christ, the result of our ministry, written not with ink but with the Spirit of the living God, not on tablets of stone but on tablets of human hearts." 2 Corinthians 3:3

MEANING

The Holy Spirit is sent by the living God to give believers life that never ends and to transform their lives.

TAKEAWAY

Life in the Spirit is dynamic and active, not static and passive.

DID YOU KNOW?

God is called the Living God because he is active in the world—rescuing and restoring those who are helpless and hopeless.

Spirit of Might

SCRIPTURE

"The Spirit of the LORD will rest on him . . . the Spirit of counsel and of might." Isaiah 11:2

MEANING

The Holy Spirit is the Spirit of strength.

TAKEAWAY

The apostle Paul explains that "the Spirit God gave us does not make us timid, but gives us power, love and self-discipline" (2 Timothy 1:7).

DID YOU KNOW?

Jesus told us he would give us the power of the Spirit (Acts 1:8).

Spirit of Prophecy

SCRIPTURE

"For it is the Spirit of prophecy who bears testimony to Jesus." Revelation 19:10

MEANING

The Spirit reveals the truth about what is and what will be.

TAKEAWAY

Because the Spirit is the source of prophecy, he can help us understand God's Word.

DID YOU KNOW?

All Scripture is inspired (God-breathed). The Spirit is the breath of inspiration (2 Timothy 3:16).

Prophecy is one of the gifts on the Spirit mentioned in Romans 12:6.

Spirit of Revelation

SCRIPTURE

"I keep asking that the God of our Lord Jesus Christ, the glorious Father, may give you the Spirit of wisdom and revelation, so that you may know him better."
Ephesians 1:17

MEANING

The Holy Spirit reveals the truth of God.

TAKEAWAY

It is the work of the Spirit to reveal God and his truth to us.

DID YOU KNOW?

Revelation comes from the Father through Jesus by the Spirit who is the voice of God in us.

Spirit of the Son

SCRIPTURE

"Because you are his sons, God sent the Spirit of his Son into our hearts, the Spirit who calls out, 'Abba, Father.'"
Galatians 4:6

MEANING

The Holy Spirit is called the Spirit of the Son because the Spirit and Jesus share the same essence and purpose.

TAKEAWAY

The loving Spirit of the Son of God is now given to us.

DID YOU KNOW?

The Spirit draws us into the love and fellowship that is between the Father and the Son.

Spirit of Truth

SCRIPTURE

"When the Advocate comes, whom I will send to you from the Father—the Spirit of truth who goes out from the Father—he will testify about me." John 15:26

MEANING

The Holy Spirit, as God, cannot lie (Titus 1:2).

TAKEAWAY

The Father and Son have given us the Spirit to lead us to truth, not error (John 16:13).

DID YOU KNOW?

Because Jesus is "the truth" (John 14:6), it follows that the Spirit he sends is the Spirit of truth.

Spirit of Understanding

SCRIPTURE

"The Spirit of the LORD will rest on him—the Spirit of wisdom and of understanding." Isaiah 11:2

MEANING

The Spirit is the source of all true discernment.

TAKEAWAY

The Spirit fully comprehends us and our needs and gives us the ability to grasp spiritual realities (1 Corinthians 2:14–16).

DID YOU KNOW?

Jesus said the Spirit would "guide [us] into all truth" (John 16:13).

Spirit of Wisdom

SCRIPTURE

"I keep asking that the God of our Lord Jesus Christ, the glorious Father, may give you the Spirit of wisdom and revelation, so that you may know him better."
Ephesians 1:17

MEANING

Because God is all-wise, and the Spirit is God in us, the Holy Spirit is able to make us wise (Romans 16:27).

TAKEAWAY

When we are filled with and led by the Spirit, we will live in wise ways.

DID YOU KNOW?

Wisdom can be described as "skill in living." It is the ability to see life and the world the way God sees them. Wisdom is practical knowledge that allows people to live fully, making godly choices.

A message of wisdom is one of the gifts of the Spirit mentioned in 1 Corinthians 12:8.

Spirit of Yahweh

SCRIPTURE

"The Spirit of the Sovereign LORD [Yahweh] is on me, because the LORD has anointed me to proclaim good news to the poor. He has sent me to bind up the brokenhearted, to proclaim freedom for the captives and release from darkness for the prisoners." Isaiah 61:1

MEANING

The Spirit has the sacred name of God: Yahweh.

TAKEAWAY

Because God is one essence, the Spirit is known as the Spirit of Yahweh.

DID YOU KNOW?

In English Bibles, *Yahweh* is often translated as LORD (with capital letters).

GIFTS OF THE SPIRIT

All the activities of the Holy Spirit—from interceding and advocating to guiding and empowering—point to his main role: to glorify Christ (John 16:14). Similarly, the goal of our own ministries should be to glorify Christ.

- How do we do this?

  By serving the body of Christ and helping it grow *up* (mature) and grow *out* (expand).

- How do we do this *most effectively*?

  Through the work of the Holy Spirit, especially his work of empowering believers—enabling and equipping each one of us with special abilities for serving.

Ministries are activities believers do that serve the church and allow it to grow and mature. Through the Holy Spirit, God gives gifts—in the sense of presents—

to each believer. These gifts are called *spiritual gifts* because they are given by the Holy Spirit (1 Corinthians 12:11). They are the tools we use to serve God and minister to others.

The Body of Christ

When Paul explained what the church is and how it works, he used the image of a body. Paul's teaching in 1 Corinthians 12 and Romans 12 speaks about the organic unity of Christ's body, the church. The Holy Spirit gives gifts with particular spiritual functions for the benefit of the entire church. The gifts complement each other and work together for the common good, much as the parts of the body are designed to do.

> "For just as each of us has one body with many members, and these members do not all have the same function, so in Christ we, though many, form one body, and each member belongs to all the others. We have different gifts, according to the grace given to each of us."
>
> **ROMANS 12:4–6**

The Holy Spirit is God's gift to us as individuals and as a body (Acts 2:38; 10:45). Individuals who have come into this life, the life of Christ, are automatically part of a larger whole. These gifts operate as parts of a whole. Gifting, reception of the Spirit, and membership in the body of Christ are all connected in the life of the believer and for the good of the whole church.

What Are Gifts?

The English word *gift* has two meanings:

1. Something that is given without a charge and freely, such as a present for a birthday.

2. A special ability or talent, such as playing piano or learning languages.

Both of these meanings help us understand spiritual gifts.

1. Spiritual gifts are unearned and undeserved. They are God's generous gifts to us!

2. Spiritual gifts involve special talents and abilities, particularly for ministries like healings, miracles, or speaking in tongues.

However, the emphasis of the New Testament is not on the abilities themselves but on how they function in the ministries (services) of the church. As we think about spiritual gifts, keep in mind that what makes them spiritual is that they come from the Holy Spirit, and what makes them a gift is that the Holy Spirit freely gives them to us. Spiritual gifts are not meant to be stored or publicized. They are meant to be used for the service of others.

Four Lists of Spiritual Gifts in the Bible

	Romans 12:6–8	1 Cor. 12:8–10	1 Cor. 12:28–30	Ephesians 4:11
Pastoring				✔
Teaching	✔		✔	✔
Encouraging (Exhortation)	✔			
Prophecy	✔	✔	✔	✔
Healings		✔	✔	
Leadership	✔			
Guidance			✔	
Message of Wisdom		✔		
Message of Knowledge		✔		
Miracles		✔	✔	
Service/Helps	✔		✔	
Acts of Mercy	✔			
Giving	✔			
Speaking in and/ or Interpreting Tongues		✔	✔	
Faith		✔		
Evangelism				✔
Distinguishing between Spirits		✔		
Apostleship			✔	✔

Pastoring, Teaching, and Encouraging
ROMANS 12:7–8; 1 COR. 12:28–29; EPH. 4:11

Traditionally, the ministry of pastors is closely connected to that of teaching. In addition to caring for the members of each church, the other crucial role of pastors is to explain the apostolic teachings to believers.

However, many people can thrive as teachers without having to become pastors. Teaching is a vital ministry of the body of Christ. Beyond giving information, teaching allows people to deepen their relationship with God and equips believers to be aware of false teachings that they might encounter.

Closely connected to other gifts, encouraging (or exhortation) means that a person comes alongside another with words of comfort, consolation, and counsel to help them be all God wants them to be.

Prophecy
ROMANS 12:6; 1 CORINTHIANS 12:10, 28;
EPHESIANS 4:11

- Prophets played an important role in the formation of the early church. Their activities included:

  - Announcing what will happen (Acts 11:28; 21:11).

  - Encouraging believers (Acts 15:32).

  - Making known the mysteries of salvation (Ephesians 3:5–6).

- Some Christians believe that the "office" of prophet ended with the close of the era of the apostles.

- In 1 Thessalonians 5:21–22 believers are told not to despise prophecy, but to "test everything" to see if it is truly from God.

- The apostle Paul reminds believers that even a gift like prophecy without love is useless (1 Corinthians 13:2).

Healings
1 CORINTHIANS 12:9, 28, 30

- Healings, like other miracles, were a demonstration of God's power that validated apostolic authority.

- The specific "office" of healer (if there was ever one) may have ended with the apostolic age.

- However, Christians continue to believe that God can and does heal as a response to prayer.

Leadership and Guidance
ROMANS 12:8; 1 CORINTHIANS 12:28

Although traditionally these gifts have been related to the ministry of elders in the church, the context of the passages suggests that they are meant for all believers.

These ministries are applicable to many areas of church life:

- Goals for the church
- Teaching
- Evangelism
- Acts of mercy and service

Message of Wisdom and Message of Knowledge
1 CORINTHIANS 12:8

We must understand these two gifts in the context of the whole letter to the Corinthians:

- The Corinthian church seems to have struggled with being too impressed with, and attracted to, the more "flashy" gifts of tongues and prophecy.

- Although Paul does not deny their importance, he makes it clear that tongues and prophecy are empty without love, wisdom, and knowledge.

Wisdom is the discerning and understanding of God's doings in the world and the way the world functions. This is a critical ministry that allows all ministries and gifts of the church to work in harmony and unity.

Knowledge allows believers to understand and explain God's revelation to others.

Miracles
1 CORINTHIANS 12:10, 28–29

For the apostle Paul, miracles existed to validate the message of the apostles: "I persevered in demonstrating among you the marks of a true apostle, including signs, wonders and miracles" (2 Corinthians 12:12).

Some examples of miracles in the New Testament are:

- The judgment of Ananias and Sapphira (Acts 5:9–11)

- The judgment of Elymas the magician (Acts 13:6–11)

Many Christians believe that the need for these miracles for validation ended with the passing of the apostles. However, Christians affirm the possibility and existence of miracles from God today.

Service/Helps, Acts of Mercy, and Giving
1 CORINTHIANS 12:28; ROMANS 12:7–8

These different gifts are so closely related that some tend to assign them to the tasks of deacons in the church. However, the overall context of these passages suggests that they are activities for all believers. These gifts are crucial for the maturity of the church.

The practice of these gifts can vary. Examples include:

- Offering help to widows, orphans, and the poor

- Giving aid for the daily activities in the church

- Discerning when individuals or groups are in need of help to carry on their ministries

"Trying to do the Lord's work in your own strength is the most confusing, exhausting, and tedious of all work. But when you are filled with the Holy Spirit, then the ministry of Jesus just flows out of you."

CORRIE TEN BOOM

Speaking in Tongues and Interpreting Tongues
1 CORINTHIANS 12:10, 28, 30

The apostle Paul did not discourage speaking in tongues—in fact, he urged the Corinthian church leaders to not forbid it (1 Corinthians 14:39). However, Paul did correct an error in the church:

- Some in the Corinthian church were too enchanted with the gift of speaking in tongues.

- Paul reminded them that speaking in tongues without love is like a "resounding gong or a clanging cymbal" (1 Corinthians 13:1).

- Paul's main concern is the edification of the church as a whole, as a body.

Today, Christians differ on whether the ministry of speaking in tongues has stopped or continues. Either way, Paul makes it clear that the unity of the body of Christ is far more important than speaking, or not speaking, in tongues.

Faith
1 CORINTHIANS 12:9

This spiritual gift of faith is not "saving faith," which every believer has (Ephesians 2:8), or the daily faith necessary for the Christian life. Instead, it is faith that complements the other gifts and allows them to be daring and active.

When the ministries of the church face odds that overwhelm most people, this faith challenges, encourages, and reminds people that we serve a powerful God who owns and controls all things!

Evangelism
EPHESIANS 4:11

- Evangelism is sharing the good news of the gospel. It is the privilege and responsibility of every believer.

- Some people have a special, God-given ability to present the message of salvation in a clear, simple, and engaging way.

- Those who fit in this ministry can provide leadership to all believers to carry out the task of evangelism.

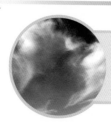

Distinguishing between Spirits
1 CORINTHIANS 12:10

In the context of the letter to the Corinthians, distinguishing (or discerning) between spirits may refer to two activities.

1. The first activity is the ability to discern when a prophecy actually comes from God. (Christians who believe that the gift of prophecy has ceased view this part of discerning as no longer necessary; see 1 Corinthians 13:8.)

2. The second activity is the ability to discern when a teaching fits in with God's will and comes from the leading of the Holy Spirit. It also includes the ability to know when a new teaching contradicts the basic teachings of the Christian faith.

Apostleship
1 CORINTHIANS 12:28–29; EPHESIANS 4:11

There is more than one kind of apostle in the
New Testament:

- The first kind refers to those Jesus called and set
  apart, who witnessed his life and ministry. These are
  the twelve disciples, and also include apostles like
  Paul and James the brother of Jesus (1 Corinthians
  9:1; 15:5–9; Galatians 2:9).

- The second kind of apostle includes those who
  were especially appointed as missionaries to spread
  the gospel—for example, Barnabas and Silas
  (Acts 13:2–3; 14:14; 15:40; 1 Thessalonians 1:1; 2:6).

Discovering Your Spiritual Gifts

When it comes to your own spiritual gifts, remember that simply knowing your gifts is not the goal. Instead, the goal is to know how to serve God and others as a member of Christ's body and then do that.

With that in mind, here are some suggestions for discerning your spiritual gifts:

- Ask God for guidance and wisdom to find your place in the church's ministry.

- Your life experience can be a good guide to find your interest and abilities.

- Be mindful of the needs of your church. Sometimes, God will call you to serve in areas you might not prefer. The calling may be temporary or long-term.

- Be ready, willing, and courageous. Obedience is challenging.

- Listen to the encouragement, wisdom, and guidance of other members of the body of Christ.

- Be prayerful about finding God's will for you.

FRUIT OF THE SPIRIT

In Galatians 5:16–25, the apostle Paul contrasts two different kinds of lives: one that allows the sinful nature ("the flesh") to lead it, and another that follows the promptings and guidance of the Holy Spirit. The life of a person whom the Spirit leads produces fruit—attitudes and behavior that are pleasing to God and other people.

"If we are full of pride and conceit and ambition and self-seeking and pleasure and the world, there is no room for the Spirit of God, and I believe many a man is praying to God to fill him when he is full already with something else."

DWIGHT L. MOODY

SINFUL NATURE	PROMPTINGS OF THE SPIRIT
The sinful nature produces attitudes and actions that oppose God's will.	The Spirit naturally leads one to attitudes and actions that are in step with the will of God.
Galatians 5:19–21	Galatians 5:22–25

"The acts of the flesh are obvious:

- sexual immorality,
- impurity and debauchery;
- idolatry and witchcraft;
- hatred,
- discord,
- jealousy,
- fits of rage,
- selfish ambition,
- dissensions,
- factions and envy;
- drunkenness,
- orgies, and the like.

I warn you, as I did before, that those who live like this will not inherit the kingdom of God."

"But the fruit of the Spirit is:

- love,
- joy,
- peace,
- patience
- kindness,
- goodness,
- faithfulness,
- gentleness and
- self-control.

Against such things there is no law. Those who belong to Christ Jesus have crucified the flesh with its passions and desires. Since we live by the Spirit, let us keep in step with the Spirit."

Love

DEFINITION

Love is not based on emotions or feelings. It is a decision to be committed to the well-being of others without any conditions or circumstances. Love seeks the highest good of others.

JESUS' EXAMPLE

Jesus said, "My command is this: Love each other as I have loved you. Greater love has no one than this: to lay down one's life for one's friends." John 15:12–13

THE HOLY SPIRIT AND LOVE

"God's love has been poured out into our hearts through the Holy Spirit, who has been given to us." Romans 5:5

Joy

DEFINITION

Joy is gladness not based on external circumstances. Biblical joy is deeper than worldly happiness. It is not based on financial success, good health, or popularity. By believing in God, obeying his will, receiving his forgiveness, participating in fellowship with other believers, ministering to others, and sharing the gospel, believers will experience joy.

JESUS' EXAMPLE

"At that time Jesus, full of joy through the Holy Spirit, said, 'I praise you, Father, Lord of heaven and earth, because you have hidden these things from the wise and learned, and revealed them to little children. Yes, Father, for this is what you were pleased to do.'" Luke 10:21

THE HOLY SPIRIT AND JOY

"The disciples were filled with joy and with the Holy Spirit." Acts 13:52

"You became imitators of us and of the Lord, for you welcomed the message in the midst of severe suffering with the joy given by the Holy Spirit." 1 Thessalonians 1:6

Peace

DEFINITION

Peace is contentment, unity between people. It is a
state of assurance and lack of fear. It is fellowship,
harmony, and unity. Peace is freedom from worry,
disturbance, and oppressive thoughts.

JESUS' EXAMPLE

*"Peace I leave with you; my peace I give you. I do not
give to you as the world gives. Do not let your hearts be
troubled and do not be afraid."* John 14:27

THE HOLY SPIRIT AND PEACE

"Keep the unity of the Spirit through the bond of peace."
Ephesians 4:3

*"The mind governed by the flesh is death, but the mind
governed by the Spirit is life and peace."* Romans 8:6

Patience

DEFINITION

Patience (or forbearance) is being slow to speak and slow to anger. It is the quality of restraint that prevents believers from speaking or acting hastily in the face of disagreement, opposition, or persecution. Patience is bearing pain or problems without complaining.

JESUS' EXAMPLE

In a letter to his friend Timothy, the apostle Paul wrote, *"Here is a trustworthy saying that deserves full acceptance: Christ Jesus came into the world to save sinners—of whom I am the worst. But for that very reason I was shown mercy so that in me, the worst of sinners, Christ Jesus might display his immense patience as an example for those who would believe in him and receive eternal life."* 1 Timothy 1:15–16

THE HOLY SPIRIT AND PATIENCE

"Be completely humble and gentle; be patient, bearing with one another in love. Make every effort to keep the unity of the Spirit through the bond of peace." Ephesians 4:2–3

"For through the Spirit we eagerly await by faith the righteousness for which we hope." Galatians 5:5

Kindness

DEFINITION

Kindness is being merciful, sweet, and tender. Kindness is an eagerness to put others at ease. It is an attractive temperament that shows friendly regard.

JESUS' EXAMPLE

"God raised us up with Christ and seated us with him in the heavenly realms in Christ Jesus, in order that in the coming ages he might show the incomparable riches of his grace, expressed in his kindness to us in Christ Jesus." Ephesians 2:6–7

"When [Jesus] saw the crowds, he had compassion on them, because they were harassed and helpless, like sheep without a shepherd." Matthew 9:36

THE HOLY SPIRIT AND KINDNESS

"But when the kindness and love of God our Savior appeared, he saved us, not because of righteous things we had done, but because of his mercy. He saved us through the washing of rebirth and renewal by the Holy Spirit." Titus 3:4–5

Goodness

DEFINITION

Goodness means being unselfish and openhearted. It is the desire to be generous to others above what they deserve.

JESUS' EXAMPLE

"God anointed Jesus of Nazareth with the Holy Spirit and power. . . . He went around doing good and healing all who were under the power of the devil, because God was with him." Acts 10:38

THE HOLY SPIRIT AND GOODNESS

"Teach me to do your will, for you are my God; may your good Spirit lead me on level ground." Psalm 143:10

"We continually ask God to fill you with the knowledge of his will through all the wisdom and understanding that the Spirit gives, so that you may live a life worthy of the Lord and please him in every way: bearing fruit in every good work." Colossians 1:9–10

Faithfulness

DEFINITION

Faithfulness means being dependable, loyal, and full of trust. Faithfulness is firm devotion to God, loyalty to friends, and dependability to carry out responsibilities. Faith is the conviction that even now God is working and acting on one's behalf.

JESUS' EXAMPLE

Jesus was faithful to the will of God the Father: *"[Jesus] withdrew about a stone's throw beyond them, knelt down and prayed, 'Father, if you are willing, take this cup from me; yet not my will, but yours be done.'"* Luke 22:41–42

"Christ is faithful as the Son over God's house. And we are his house, if indeed we hold firmly to our confidence and the hope in which we glory." Hebrews 3:6

THE HOLY SPIRIT AND FAITHFULNESS

"When you believed, you were marked in him with a seal, the promised Holy Spirit, who is a deposit guaranteeing our inheritance until the redemption of those who are God's possession." Ephesians 1:13–14

Gentleness

DEFINITION

Gentleness is being humble, calm, and non-threatening. A gentle demeanor is rooted in a position of strength and authority, and is useful in calming another's anger. Gentleness is not a quality that is weak and passive.

JESUS' EXAMPLE

"Come to me, all you who are weary and burdened, and I will give you rest. Take my yoke upon you and learn from me, for I am gentle and humble in heart, and you will find rest for your souls. For my yoke is easy and my burden is light." Matthew 11:28–30

THE HOLY SPIRIT AND GENTLENESS

"If someone is caught in a sin, you who live by the Spirit should restore that person gently." Galatians 6:1

"Since we live by the Spirit, let us keep in step with the Spirit. Let us not become conceited, provoking and envying each other." Galatians 5:25–26

Self-control

DEFINITION

Self-control means to restrain one's emotions, actions, and desires, and to be in harmony with the will of God. Self-control is doing God's will, not living for one's self.

JESUS' EXAMPLE

"When [Jesus' accusers] hurled their insults at him, he did not retaliate; when he suffered, he made no threats. Instead, he entrusted himself to him who judges justly." 1 Peter 2:23

THE HOLY SPIRIT AND SELF-CONTROL

"Walk by the Spirit, and you will not gratify the desires of the flesh." Galatians 5:16

"For the Spirit God gave us does not make us timid, but gives us power, love and self-discipline." 2 Timothy 1:7

How Do We Pray in the Spirit?

"Praying in the Spirit" is mentioned two times in the New Testament: Ephesians 6:18 and Jude 20. To pray in the Spirit means to pray according to the Spirit's promptings and guidance. When we allow our prayers to be led by the Holy Spirit we pray in accordance with God's will.

> "Prayer is an art which only the Spirit can teach us. He is the giver of all prayer."
>
> **CHARLES SPURGEON**

The Spirit of God is the Spirit of prayer. Jesus promised the presence of the Spirit in the life of his disciples (John 14:16–17). One of the crucial tasks of the Holy Spirit is to inspire and guide our prayers. When our weaknesses prevent us from relating to God correctly, the Spirit intercedes for us—that is, he pleads our case before God:

> *"In the same way, the Spirit helps us in our weakness. We do not know what we ought to pray for, but the Spirit himself intercedes for us through wordless groans. And he who searches our hearts knows the mind of the Spirit, because the Spirit intercedes for God's people in accordance with the will of God."* Romans 8:26–27

We can rest assured that the Spirit is praying alongside us, making our prayers what they ought to be.

Dialogue, Not Monologue

If we understand prayer as communication with God, then we will be able to see it more fully as a dialogue, rather than a monologue on our part. Prayer is a two-way conversation; the other half of our worship before God is God's guidance and clarity of his will to us. Just as we may only reach God in the Spirit through the truth of Christ (John 4:24), so also God's guidance and teaching comes to us only through Christ by means of the Spirit (John 14:26; 15:26; 16:12–14).

What Is Blasphemy Against the Holy Spirit?

Jesus said, "People can be forgiven all their sins and every slander they utter, but whoever blasphemes against the Holy Spirit will never be forgiven" (Mark 3:28–29).

The issue of blasphemy against the Spirit has bothered many Bible readers. Blasphemy involves an utterance or action that purposefully defames God. Blasphemies against God are prohibited in the third commandment (Exodus 20:7), yet people regularly misuse God's name and are forgiven. Jesus' name is a target of abuse, yet Christ himself teaches that these offenses may be forgiven (Luke 12:10). What makes blasphemy of the Holy Spirit different?

- Jesus seems to be speaking about something bigger than mere words or actions directed against God's Spirit.

- The context helps us to see that what Jesus' accusers were involved in was insisting that Jesus' Spirit (the Holy Spirit) was at the core demonic, satanic, evil (Mark 3:30)!

■ The point seems to be not that the name calling itself could not be forgiven, but that the ramifications of their words would cause the speakers to reject God's only offer of salvation.

Why? Because the Holy Spirit is God's final witness to Christ and his salvation. If the whisper of the Spirit in the ear or the shout of his voice in creation and history is ignored fully and finally, there can be no forgiveness, because there will be no regeneration, no conversion, no repentance.

Blasphemy of the Holy Spirit is thus tied to one of the Spirit's most important works—revelation. In the end, it is the Spirit of Truth, the Spirit of Revelation, who must turn the minds and hearts of the human race.

What Is Baptism of the Holy Spirit?

The literal meaning of the word *baptism* is "to immerse" or "to dip in or under." Some Christians believe that the baptism of the Holy Spirit (or baptism *in* or *with* the Holy Spirit) occurs at the moment of salvation. That is, when a person trusts in Christ, the Spirit places them "in Christ" or immerses them in his body (1 Corinthians 12:13). This event may or may not be accompanied by some sort of outward expression. In this view, the secondary act of undergoing water baptism (also called believer's baptism) acts as a powerful external expression of this inward spiritual reality.

Other Christians believe that baptism of the Holy Spirit happens after salvation. That is, it's a special "second blessing" given by God to empower people for service and growth in the faith (Matthew 3:11; Acts 1:5; 2:33, 38).

Whatever view one holds, this much is clear: Just as water baptism serves as a kind of initiation into the Christian life and identifies one as a follower of Jesus, in the same way, those of us who have experienced the baptism of the Spirit should live lives that show we are "in Christ." In the way we think, talk, decide, interact, work, play—do we demonstrate our identification with Christ? Do we look to the Lord, and to his Spirit, for power to live in ways that bring honor to him and blessing to others?

Can a Christian Lose the Holy Spirit?

No, someone who has put their trust in Jesus as Savior cannot "lose" the Holy Spirit. God has given us the Spirit as a "seal" and a "deposit guaranteeing our inheritance" (Ephesians 1:13–14). The Holy Spirit is our guarantee that God will make good on his promise of eternal life for all who come to him through Christ.

In Old Testament times, God gave his Spirit to particular individuals for service—and sometimes removed the Spirit if an individual sinned. For example, David prayed in Psalm 51:11, "Do not cast me from your presence or take your Holy Spirit from me." In the New Testament, however, the Holy Spirit is promised to all believers in Jesus permanently (John 14:16).

What Does It Mean to Grieve the Spirit?

In Ephesians 4:30, the apostle Paul urges believers, "Do not grieve the Holy Spirit of God." This indicates the personhood of the Holy Spirit; a thing, an "it," cannot feel sorrow.

So how do we avoid grieving the Holy Spirit in us? The context of verse 30 gives us a clue. Here, the apostle Paul is reminding believers to:

- Watch what we say ("no unwholesome talk," "slander," "only what is helpful," verse 29).

- Avoid becoming bitter, angry people ("Get rid of all bitterness, rage, brawling" verses 29, 31).

- Treat others like Christ does ("kind, compassionate, forgiving," verse 32).

When we behave sinfully—particularly when we treat others in un-Christlike ways—this grieves the Holy Spirit. This is the opposite of the fruits of the Spirit that he wants to grow in our lives.

What Does It Mean to Quench the Spirit?

Paul cautions believers in his letter to the Thessalonians: "Do not quench the Spirit" (1 Thessalonians 5:19). The imagery is that of a fire being put out—quenched. Some Bible versions translate the word *quench* as stifle, suppress, or restrain.

Immediately after Paul warns believers not to quench the Spirit, he says, "Do not treat prophecies with contempt but test them all; hold on to what is good, reject every kind of evil" (verses 20–22). When we see the work of the Holy Spirit in our lives and the lives of other believers and we try to stop it, suppress it, or dismiss it, we are quenching the Spirit.

> "Breathe in me, O Holy Spirit, that my thoughts may all be holy. Act in me, O Holy Spirit, that my work, too, may be holy. Draw my heart, O Holy Spirit, that I love but what is holy. Strengthen me, O Holy Spirit, to defend all that is holy. Guard me, then, O Holy Spirit, that I always may be holy."
>
> **AUGUSTINE**

It's not wrong to be cautious. In fact, Paul says to "test them all" and "reject every kind of evil." But when we see the good work of the Holy Spirit, we should always "hold to what is good" (verse 21).

MADE EASY

by Rose Publishing

The *Made Easy* series helps you quickly find biblical answers to important questions. These pocket-sized books are packed with clear explanations and key facts you need to know.

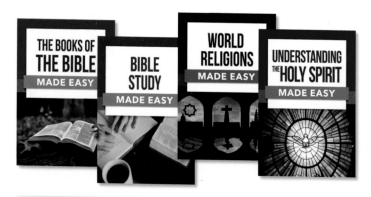

THE BOOKS OF THE BIBLE MADE EASY
Quick summaries of all 66 books of the Bible
ISBN 9781628623420

BIBLE STUDY MADE EASY
A step-by-step guide to studying God's Word
ISBN 9781628623437

WORLD RELIGIONS MADE EASY
30 religions and how they compare to Christianity
ISBN 9781628623451

UNDERSTANDING THE HOLY SPIRIT MADE EASY
Who the Holy Spirit is and what he does
ISBN 9781628623444

 HENDRICKSON PUBLISHERS ROSE PUBLISHING

www.hendricksonrose.com

THE AGATHA CHRISTIE COLLECTION

The Man in the Brown Suit
The Secret of Chimneys
The Seven Dials Mystery
The Mysterious Mr. Quin
The Sittaford Mystery
Parker Pyne Investigates
Why Didn't They Ask Evans?
Murder Is Easy
The Regatta Mystery and Other
Stories
And Then There Were None
Towards Zero
Death Comes as the End
Sparkling Cyanide
The Witness for the Prosecution
and Other Stories
Crooked House
Three Blind Mice and Other
Stories
They Came to Baghdad
Destination Unknown
Ordeal by Innocence
Double Sin and Other Stories
The Pale Horse
Star over Bethlehem: Poems and
Holiday Stories
Endless Night
Passenger to Frankfurt
The Golden Ball and Other Stories
The Mousetrap and Other Plays
The Harlequin Tea Set

The Hercule Poirot Mysteries

The Mysterious Affair at Styles
The Murder on the Links
Poirot Investigates
The Murder of Roger Ackroyd
The Big Four
The Mystery of the Blue Train
Peril at End House
Lord Edgware Dies
Murder on the Orient Express
Three Act Tragedy
Death in the Clouds
The A.B.C. Murders
Murder in Mesopotamia
Cards on the Table
Murder in the Mews and
Other Stories

Dumb Witness
Death on the Nile
Appointment with Death
Hercule Poirot's Christmas
Sad Cypress
One, Two, Buckle My Shoe
Evil Under the Sun
Five Little Pigs
The Hollow
The Labors of Hercules
Taken at the Flood
The Underdog and Other Stories
Mrs. McGinty's Dead
After the Funeral
Hickory Dickory Dock
Dead Man's Folly
Cat Among the Pigeons
The Clocks
Third Girl
Hallowe'en Party
Elephants Can Remember
Curtain: Poirot's Last Case

The Miss Marple Mysteries

The Murder at the Vicarage
The Body in the Library
The Moving Finger
A Murder Is Announced
They Do It with Mirrors
A Pocket Full of Rye
4:50 from Paddington
The Mirror Crack'd from
Side to Side
A Caribbean Mystery
At Bertram's Hotel
Nemesis
Sleeping Murder
Miss Marple: The Complete
Short Story Collection

The Tommy and Tuppence Mysteries

The Secret Adversary
Partners in Crime
N or M?
By the Pricking of My Thumbs
Postern of Fate